Biggest, Baddest Books for Boys

Biggest, Baddest Book of
DINOSAURS

Anders Hanson & Elissa Mann

Consulting Editor, Diane Craig, M.A./Reading Specialist

A Division of ABDO

ABDO
Publishing Company

visit us at www.abdopublishing.com

Published by ABDO Publishing Company, a division of ABDO, P.O. Box 398166, Minneapolis, Minnesota 55439. Copyright © 2013 by Abdo Consulting Group, Inc. International copyrights reserved in all countries. No part of this book may be reproduced in any form without written permission from the publisher. Super SandCastle™ is a trademark and logo of ABDO Publishing Company.

Printed in the United States of America, North Mankato, Minnesota
062012
062013

 PRINTED ON RECYCLED PAPER

Editor: Liz Salzmann
Content Developer: Nancy Tuminelly
Cover and Interior Design and Production: Anders Hanson, Mighty Media, Inc.
Illustration Credits: Nobumichi Tamura, Shutterstock

Library of Congress Cataloging-in-Publication Data
Hanson, Anders, 1980-
 Biggest, baddest book of dinosaurs / Anders Hanson and Elissa Mann.
     p. cm. -- (Biggest, baddest books for boys)
 ISBN 978-1-61783-406-6 (alk. paper)
 1. Dinosaurs--Juvenile literature. I. Mann, Elissa. II. Title.
 QE861.5.H364 2013
 567.9--dc23
                         2011050918

Super SandCastle™ books are created by a team of professional educators, reading specialists, and content developers around five essential components—phonemic awareness, phonics, vocabulary, text comprehension, and fluency—to assist young readers as they develop reading skills and strategies and increase their general knowledge. All books are written, reviewed, and leveled for guided reading, early reading intervention, and Accelerated Reader® programs for use in shared, guided, and independent reading and writing activities to support a balanced approach to literacy instruction.

CONTENTS

DINO-MIGHT

Dinosaurs were some of the scariest creatures ever! *Dinosaur* means "terrible lizard." Sometimes we call them *dinos* for short.

Dinos lived millions of years ago. Most of them died out long ago. But they left behind a lot of bones. We can learn about dinos by looking at their bones!

WHAT WERE DINOSAURS?

Dinosaurs were reptiles. They had backbones and laid eggs. They had thick, tough skin.

Dinos came in many shapes and sizes. Some were huge plant-eaters. Others were terrifying meat-eaters.

Some dinos walked on two feet. Others walked on all fours. And some dinos could even fly! Did you know that birds are a type of dinosaur?

HOW ARE DINOS DISCOVERED?

The bones are dug up. They are put together to make a skeleton.

First the bones are found. They are usually buried underground.

Then we study the skeleton. We try to figure out how the dino looked and acted.

5

DINOSAUR FAMILY TREE

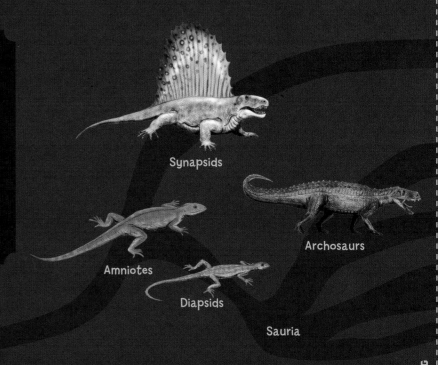

Dinos ruled the land. But they were not alone.

This chart shows dinos and their relatives. Can you see how they are connected? All of these animals had a common **ancestor**. It was a type of fish!

Synapsids

Archosaurs

Amniotes

Diapsids

Sauria

Tetrapods

AMPHIBIANS

THE GREAT DYING

The Great Dying was a mass extinction. Many types of animals died out. The Great Dying killed more animals than any other event ever. It cleared the way for dinos to take over the Earth.

Lobe-Finned Fishes

THE GREAT DYING

DEVONIAN PERIOD
(416–359 MILLION YEARS AGO)

CARBONIFEROUS PERIOD
(359–299 MILLION YEARS AGO)

PERMIAN PERIOD
(299–251 MILLION YEARS AGO)

Pterosaurs

BIRDS

MAMMALS

Coelurosaurs

Ceratosaurs

Velociraptors

Dinosaurs

Sauropods

CROCODILES

Theropods

Stegosauria

Tyrannosaurids

LIZARDS
AND SNAKES

Ornithischia

Ceratopsia

Ankylosauria

THE END OF THE DINOSAURS

Ichthyosaurs

Plesiosaurs

THE END OF THE DINOSAURS
Another mass extinction happened
65 million years ago. All of the dinos
died except for some birds.

TRIASSIC PERIOD
(251-199 MILLION YEARS AGO)

JURASSIC PERIOD
(199-145 MILLION YEARS AGO)

CRETACEOUS PERIOD
(145-65 MILLION YEARS AGO)

EVOLUTION

CREATURES CHANGE SLOWLY OVER TIME.
OVER MILLIONS OF YEARS, SOME
ANIMALS DEVELOP NEW ABILITIES!

Before the age of dinosaurs, the oceans were full of fish. Some fish grew limbs that helped them walk on land.

Some dinosaurs could fly. *Archaeopteryx* may have been one of the first. It had wings and feathers. But unlike modern birds, it had sharp teeth. It also had fingers!

FEATHERED DINOS?

Many raptor dinos had feathers. Some even had feathers on their legs! They could use their legs like a second pair of wings! They could probably glide, but not fly.

Microraptor

THE BIGGEST AND SMALLEST

THE BIGGEST DINOSAURS WERE THE LARGEST LAND ANIMALS EVER TO WALK THE EARTH!

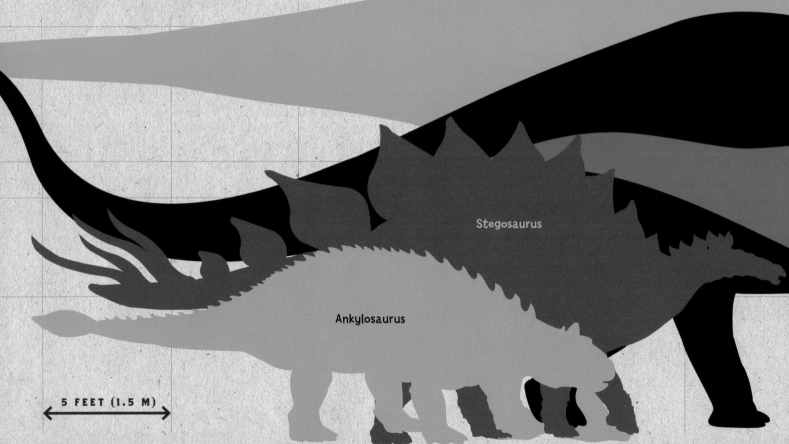

Stegosaurus

Ankylosaurus

5 FEET (1.5 M)

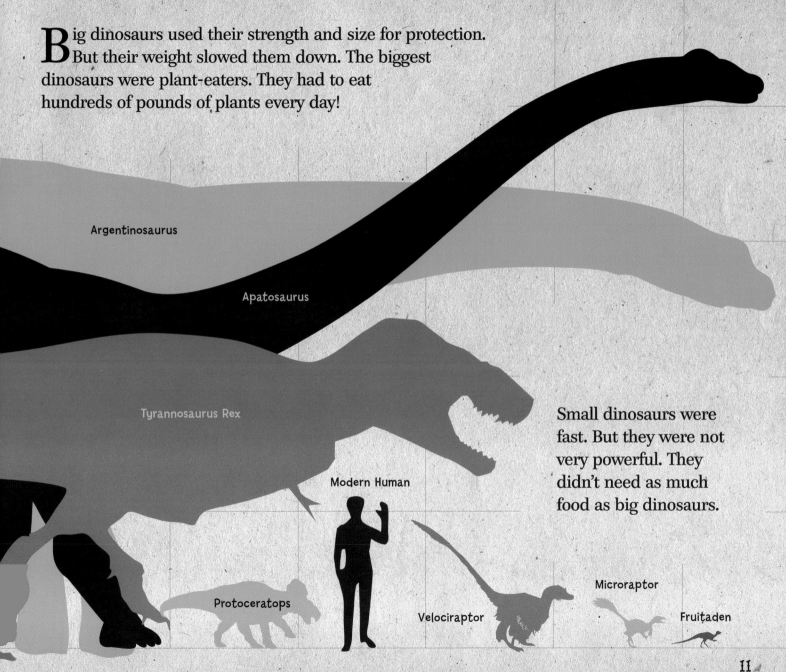

Big dinosaurs used their strength and size for protection. But their weight slowed them down. The biggest dinosaurs were plant-eaters. They had to eat hundreds of pounds of plants every day!

Argentinosaurus

Apatosaurus

Tyrannosaurus Rex

Modern Human

Small dinosaurs were fast. But they were not very powerful. They didn't need as much food as big dinosaurs.

Protoceratops

Velociraptor

Microraptor

Fruitaden

11

ARE YOU *FASTER*

Could you outrun a dino? The answer depends on the dinosaur.

Four-legged dinos couldn't move fast. Many had short legs. Their heavy bodies slowed them down.

Two-legged dinos were fast. They had long legs. Long tails helped them balance.

STEGOSAURUS

4 MILES PER HOUR (6 KPH)

APATOSAURUS

12 MILES PER HOUR (19 KPH)

TRICERATOPS
16 MILES PER HOUR (26 KPH)

MODERN HUMAN ATHLETE

17 MILES PER HOUR (27 KPH)

TYRANNOSAURUS
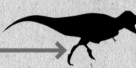
18 MILES PER HOUR (29 KPH)

VELOCIRAPTOR
24 MILES PER HOUR (39 KPH)

COMPSOGNATHUS
40 MILES PER HOUR (64 KPH)

THAN A DINO?

HOW DO WE KNOW?

Dinosaurs left behind footprints! We can measure the space between the prints. Then we can guess how fast they moved.

SPEED CHAMP

Compsognathus was a really fast dinosaur. It was about the size of the average house cat. Its thin, **flexible** body let it move quickly.

KILLING MACHINES

CLEAVER CLAWS

Many meat-eating dinos had huge claws. They were perfect for ripping and tearing. *Velociraptor* had a giant claw on each back foot.

TEETH FOR TEARING

Meat-eaters had a lot of sharp teeth. They used them to rip their food apart. *T-Rex* had 50 to 60 teeth.

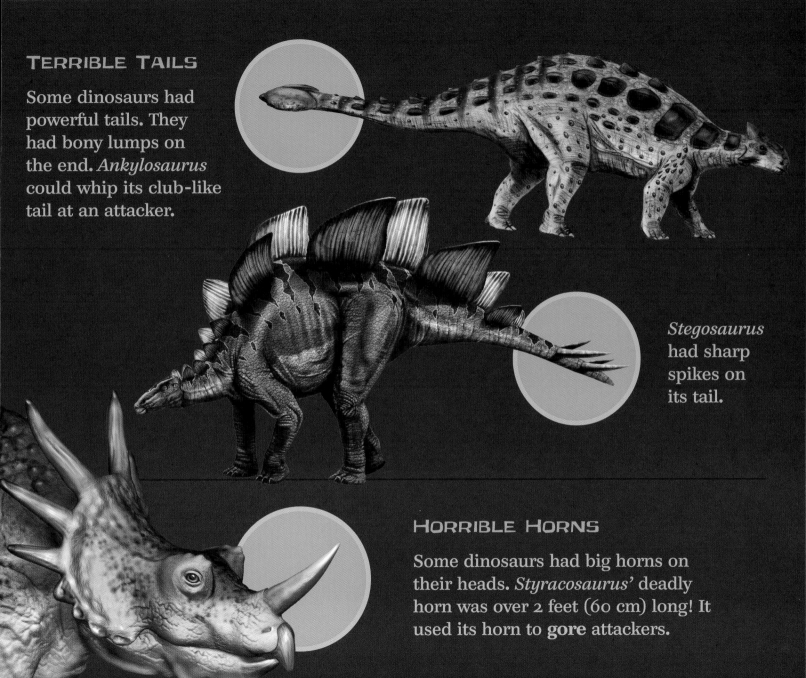

TERRIBLE TAILS

Some dinosaurs had powerful tails. They had bony lumps on the end. *Ankylosaurus* could whip its club-like tail at an attacker.

Stegosaurus had sharp spikes on its tail.

HORRIBLE HORNS

Some dinosaurs had big horns on their heads. *Styracosaurus'* deadly horn was over 2 feet (60 cm) long! It used its horn to **gore** attackers.

FOUR-LEGGED TANKS

Some dinosaurs had their very own suits of armor. Layers of bone and tough skin covered their bodies. Spikes and spines stuck out from their backs. Some had spikes on their shoulders and heads too. They were hard to eat!

THICK SKIN

Armored dinos had thick, rough skin. It was tough like leather. Their skin was really hard to bite through! It may have been like crocodile or ostrich skin.

crocodile skin

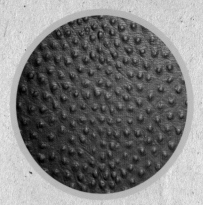
ostrich skin

SCALY SCUTES

Scutes were small, bony bumps under dino skin. They were a lot like scales. But they didn't cover the whole body.

SPIKY SPINES

Spines stuck out from the sides of these dinos. They protected the dinos from attackers.

GIANTS
IN THE
SKY

crests

P terosaurs were the first flying animals with backbones. *Pterosaur* means "winged lizard." They were not true dinosaurs. But they were related to them.

Many pterosaurs had colorful crests on their heads.

18

Pterosaurs could fly fast! They swooped through the sky at up to 30 miles per hour (50 kph).

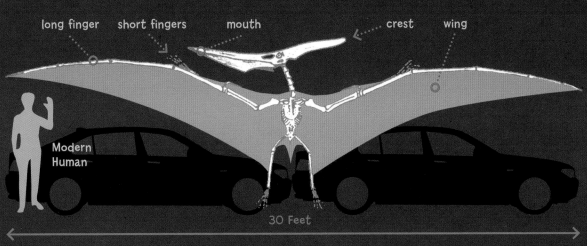

long finger   short fingers   mouth   crest   wing

Modern Human

30 Feet

Pterosaurs were the largest flying creatures ever. Some had **wingspans** of 30 to 36 feet (9 to 11 m). That's about the length of two cars!

MONSTERS

THESE SEA MONSTERS LIVED DURING THE TIME OF THE DINOSAURS

Nothosaurs lived partly in water and partly on land. Their needle-sharp teeth were perfect for tearing apart fish and squid.

Nothosaurus

Tylosaurus was up to 49 feet (15m) long. It used its long **snout** to ram turtles and fish.

Tylosaurus

of the DEEP

Elasmosaurus

Elasmosaurus was a plesiosaur. It was a slow swimmer. It had a really **sensitive** nose. It could sniff out food underwater!

Ichthyosaurs had huge eyes. The eyeball was up to 10 inches (25 cm) wide! They used their great eyesight to catch food at night.

Ichthyosaurs

WHAT KILLED THE DINOSAURS?

Most dinosaurs disappeared 65 million years ago. Scientists believe that a large asteroid hit the Earth at that time. The crash caused giant fires, earthquakes, and floods. It also threw tons of earth high into the sky. This made a dark cloud that blocked the sun. The Earth got really cold without the sun!

Most dinosaurs couldn't live in the cold. Almost all of them died. Birds were the only true dinos to survive.

WHAT DO YOU KNOW ABOUT DINOS?

1. DINOSAUR MEANS "TERRIBLE LIZARD." **TRUE OR FALSE?**

2. SMALL DINOSAURS WERE USUALLY SLOW. **TRUE OR FALSE?**

3. STEGOSAURUS HAD SPIKES ON ITS TAIL. **TRUE OR FALSE?**

4. PTEROSAURS WERE TRUE DINOSAURS. **TRUE OR FALSE?**

ANSWERS: 1) TRUE 2) FALSE 3) TRUE 4) FALSE

23

GLOSSARY

ANCESTOR – a related person or animal that lived in the past.

FLEXIBLE – easy to move or bend.

GORE – to pierce or stab.

SENSITIVE – able to feel and respond to slight changes.

SNOUT – the jaws and nose of an animal.

WINGSPAN – the distance from one wing tip to the other when the wings are fully spread.